Original title:
Meaning: Always a Step Ahead of Me

Copyright © 2025 Creative Arts Management OÜ
All rights reserved.

Author: Milo Harrington
ISBN HARDBACK: 978-1-80566-236-5
ISBN PAPERBACK: 978-1-80566-531-1

Caravans of Concepts in Flight

In the land of thoughts, they dance about,
Ideas on stilts, there's never a doubt.
Like balloons at a fair, they float and sway,
Elusive and silly, they bounce away.

Juggling with wisdom, I drop the ball,
Chasing a notion, I trip and fall.
A squirrel in my brain, it steals my snack,
While thoughts of grand plans skitter off track.

Puns and quirks, they spin and twirl,
Witty remarks make my mind whirl.
A treasure map inked with giggles and grins,
But where do I start? Oh, let the fun begin!

I wave to the shadows, they wave back slow,
With a nod and a wink, they certainly know.
Though I may stumble, I laugh all the same,
For life's a big circus, and I'm in the game.

The Elusive Essence of Insight

I chased a thought, it took a jog,
And left behind a puzzled dog.
It laughed at me, a playful game,
While I just whispered, 'What's its name?'

I tried to catch it in a net,
But thoughts are sly, they won't forget.
They sneak around, they tilt and sway,
And leave me wondering every day.

Station of Awareness

At the station where ideas wait,
I missed my train, I'm running late.
A comical sign points left and right,
But none of it feels truly bright.

The conductor winks, takes my ticket,
I shake my head, feel quite a nitwit.
He giggles softly, 'It's all a game,'
I scratch my head, 'What's to blame?'

The Journey of Unfinished Thoughts

My thoughts packed bags, they hit the road,
Without a map, they shared a code.
They stopped for snacks, got sidetracked too,
In search of schemes, but found just stew.

I waved at clouds, they waved right back,
With a confusing plan, all out of whack.
They floated high, then plopped in trees,
And giggled down like cheeky bees.

Riddles Wrapped in Silence

A silence spoke, it told a joke,
I laughed so hard, my sides went broke.
But when I asked, 'What was the punch?'
The silence grinned, and ate my lunch.

With riddles wrapped in clever thought,
I brewed a tea that meant a lot.
But every sip was just a breeze,
And left me staring, feeling teased.

Shadows Dancing on the Path

In the corner of my sight, they twirl,
Chasing thoughts that spin and whirl.
They giggle softly, just out of reach,
Dancing in shadows, a playful breach.

With each trip, a laugh and a tease,
Taunting me like a playful breeze.
I chase them down, only to find,
Their steps are light, and they're unconfined.

Like cheeky sprites, they flit and hover,
Just when I'm close, they find their cover.
I stumble forward, they laugh and flee,
Even the shadows mock my decree.

But oh, what fun in this merry chase,
These shadows bring a smile to my face.
With every leap and every misstep,
A giggling partner in this jest we prep.

The Elusive Nature of Knowing

I ask the wise, they scratch their heads,
Their answers dance like strange threads.
With every clue, it slips away,
Like trying to pet a cat mid-play.

Understanding peers from behind a tree,
Hiding, giggling mischievously.
When I reach for grasp, it makes a dash,
Leaving me with just a silly splash.

In riddles spun like cotton candy,
The truth hides, so jolly and dandy.
I seek to know, it plays hide-and-seek,
Every answer feels more like a streak.

Yet there's humor in this quest of mine,
The chase is sweet, like ripe moonshine.
For in the chase, laughter does grow,
And perhaps that's the best way to know.

Whispers from the Abyss of Knowing

Down in the depths, where silence sings,
Whispers echo, pulling on strings.
I lean in close, they giggle so near,
Yet when I listen, they disappear.

"Hey, come back!" I cry to the void,
These airy thoughts seem so coy.
Each answer rolls like a runaway ball,
Just when I think I have them all.

A game of tag with the cosmos fair,
I reach for truths that dance like air.
They call out softly, then slip away,
Leaving me guessing, come what may.

But laughter rings in this curious plight,
Chasing shadows in the starlit night.
And maybe in jest, I'll catch a clue,
If I chase it down with a dance or two.

A Footrace with Revelation

On a track lined with questions galore,
I sprint ahead, but it's a chore.
With every stride, a revelation shines,
Yet it teases like candy on vines.

I run so fast, yet it blurs ahead,
Like a cheeky friend, it won't be misled.
It giggles at labels I can't apply,
Flashing wonders, as it flits by.

I pick up pace, fueled by my greed,
This race, oh how it plants the seed.
But just as I think I've reached the goal,
It tumbles down, just a playful scroll.

A friendly duel, this chase of the mind,
In the laughter of learning, joy I find.
For every twist, a giggle or two,
This footrace shows more than a clue.

Fleeting Glimpses of Purpose

I chase my thoughts like squirrels in trees,
They giggle and dart, they do as they please.
Just when I think I've caught one at last,
It hops away fast, oh how time flies past.

A sign says 'focus,' but where's the fun?
My goals do a dance, then they're on the run.
With every new plan, I'm running a race,
Yet all I collect are smiles on my face.

The Puzzle of Life's Design

I piece together bits of my day,
A corner here and there, what do they say?
With edges that don't quite fit where they go,
I laugh at the chaos, it's all just for show.

Searching for pieces, they hide and they peek,
A jigsaw of joy, with humor so chic.
I might never finish, but that's not the goal,
The fun's in the hunt, it's good for my soul.

Navigating the Waters of Intuition

I sail on a boat made of whims and of wishes,
With maps drawn by dreams and the thought of good dishes.
The navigation's tricky, oh where should I steer?
Well, toss in a fish, it anchors my fear.

My compass spins wildly, but what does it mean?
It points to my heart, the quirkiest scene.
With laughter for wind, I sail to the beat,
All laughs and no worries, oh, what a treat!

The Mirage of Certainty

I see a clear path, but it shimmers and shakes,
Like a mirage of cookies, I dream of high stakes.
Each step that I take leads me round and about,
In a fun house of thoughts, I twist and I shout.

Certainty's a jester in a patchwork of light,
Playing tricks with my brain, oh what a delight!
With giggles I'm learning, it's all part of the game,
For nothing's for sure, and life's just the same.

Navigating the Labyrinth of Intention

In a maze of thoughts, I twirl and twist,
Intentions hide, like a magician's mist.
Searching for purpose, I trip and fall,
Is it a goal or just a paintball?

Hurdles to Hallucinations

Jumping over doubts, like a circus clown,
My hopes take flight, then plummet down.
I laugh at shadows dancing in the dark,
Am I chasing dreams or just chasing a lark?

Unraveling the Tapestry of Perception

Threads of thought, all tangled and frayed,
Each one a puzzle, like a hat that's displayed.
I stitch a story, it rips at the seam,
Is it art or just a ridiculous dream?

When Tomorrow Just Outruns Us

Tomorrow's winning, I can't catch a break,
It sprints ahead, while I trip on a rake.
Time's a prankster, wearing a grin,
Who knew that the future could run with such spin?

Capturing the Wind of Knowledge

I tried to catch a breeze today,
But it giggled and slipped away.
I grabbed my net, with great big dreams,
But it just danced, bursting at the seams.

I followed paths with twists and bends,
Chasing whispers, making new friends.
It teased me with a whirl and spin,
While I just stumbled, laughing within.

I jotted notes while running fast,
But they vanished, gone in a blast.
The cloud of wisdom swirled with glee,
As I sat back, sipping iced tea.

Yet here I stand, a joyful clown,
With thoughts dashed like leaves falling down.
The wind may play a cheeky game,
But here I twirl, in joyful shame.

Just Beyond the Veil of Thought

I peeked beyond a curtain thin,
To see what thoughts might lie within.
A giggle floated, sly and bright,
As reason tickled my brain at night.

Each idea danced a merry jig,
But they vanished quick, oh what a rig!
I chased them down with nets and pails,
Yet caught a shadow, dust, and tales.

I thought I had a brilliant plan,
To capture wisdom like a can.
But logic winked before I could,
And slipped away, just like it should.

In this mad pursuit of thoughts so spry,
I wave goodbye with a cheerful sigh.
For though they tease and whirl in flight,
They leave me laughing day and night.

In Pursuit of the Unattainable

I pursued a dream on a runaway train,
But it giggled and danced, causing me pain.
With ticket in hand, I searched high and low,
Only to find it was all for show.

I set my sights on a distant star,
But it blinked and said, 'You've come too far!'
I grabbed a lasso, swung it in vain,
While the cosmos just chuckled at my gain.

Invisible treasures, they shimmer and shine,
Yet every time, they leave me behind.
I pack my bags with hope and cheer,
But they vanish like mist, gone from near.

Still, I chase with a grin and a song,
For the chase itself is where I belong.
Each unattainable dream leads me on,
With laughter and whimsy from dusk till dawn.

The Horizon Always Beckons

The horizon called, with its cheeky grin,
I raced toward it, fueled by whim.
But the more I ran, the farther it flew,
Like a game of tag, with no rendezvous.

I packed my bags with maps and dreams,
And set off to conquer, or so it seems.
But every bend held a funny surprise,
Like rain in my face and sun in my eyes.

I waved at valleys, kissed the sky,
Yet the horizon just winked, oh my!
With a playful laugh, it teased me near,
While I stumbled out loud, face red with cheer.

So here I stand, in the golden glow,
With horizons that beckon, yet follow me slow.
I'll dance with the sunsets and sing to the moon,
For chasing horizons makes me swoon.

Floating Between Clarity and Chaos

I search for sense in breakfast cereal,
But come up short—it's all just aural.
My latte whispers secrets of the day,
While my toast just crumbles, goes astray.

Floating in thoughts like balloons in air,
One pops with a laugh, and I'm left to stare.
Socks go missing in the laundry hum,
And wisdom's just a distant, silly drum.

I tickle my brain with half-baked plots,
Ideas dart by like speedy little tots.
The cat eye-rolls as I ponder deep,
She knows that clarity's lost in sleep.

Yet in the jigsaw of my scattered mind,
Laughter echoes, a reward I find.
Chaos, my friend, is a merry dance,
Where clarity shines in a fleeting glance.

The Wait for Understanding

I've been queuing for meaning at the café,
But all I got was a cold soufflé.
Patience is served, though my brain's on fire,
As the barista winks, 'You'll have to inquire.'

The clock keeps ticking, feasting on my thought,
A line of confusion that time forgot.
Wisdom walks by in a bright, silly hat,
While I'm just left wondering where she's at.

I tried to catch the bus to insight,
But it drove off with motion, out of sight.
I waved at the driver with hopeful glee,
But all that I saw was a wrong turn for me.

Yet lo and behold, in the chaos I stand,
Laughing at life with a snack in my hand.
Understanding—like cheese on a crumpet—
Is surely arriving, but still—where's my trumpet?

The Cerebral Tightrope Walk

I'm balancing on thoughts like a circus act,
With one shoe on clarity, the other abstract.
My brain does somersaults, flips through the air,
It's an acrobatic show—and I'm just a chair.

Juggling ideas like oranges in flight,
One falls on my head, it's quite the sight.
Philosophy's fine, but it's hard to digest,
Like eating spaghetti in a giant contest.

I'm teetering high on the wire of doubt,
While friends are below, cheer and shout.
"Just don't look down!" they laugh and tease,
But all that's below are my wobbly knees.

Yet the thrill of the walk keeps me smiling bright,
Amidst all the chaos and topsy delight.
I'll keep on my toes, for it's all in good fun,
As clarity giggles, "You're almost the one!"

Cyclones of Uncertainty

Whirlwinds of questions twist and twirl,
In the eye of the storm, ideas unfurl.
A tornado of thoughts that circle my head,
It's chaos, my friend, where clarity fled.

I'm swept off my feet by logic's own flight,
While confusion spins me into the night.
"Which way is up?" I scream with a grin,
As the cat rolls her eyes, "You're at it again."

I ride on a cyclone, a carnival ride,
With laughter as fuel and fear set aside.
The landscape shifts wildly, but I raise my hand,
To waves of understanding that drift like sand.

Yet amidst the storms, come rainbows of glee,
In the chaos of thought, there's a chuckle from me.
For meaning may wander, but oh what a spree,
Cyclones of uncertainty dance joyfully.

Chasing Shadows of Clarity

I chase the sun but trip on dusk,
It always seems to tease and rust.
A little light can play a trick,
While I just try to solve the flick.

The clocks all giggle, a silent cheer,
As I run laps, they disappear.
With every step, they dance away,
I laugh out loud, it's all a play!

The shadows wiggle, laugh, and twirl,
I'm pulling threads in this mad whirl.
With every twinkle, they slip and slide,
Just quite the challenge, a funny ride!

So here I am, an endless chase,
With shadows swapping all their grace.
I take a break, just need a drink,
While clarity gives me time to think!

The Elusive Essence

I ask the breeze for solid ground,
It giggles, floating all around.
With every question, it drags its feet,
Leaving me dizzy, what a feat!

An essence wrapped in tinfoil dreams,
I'm peeling layers, or so it seems.
Just when I think I've cracked the code,
That silly essence goes and explodes!

It whispers hints like a playful sprite,
In riddles that keep me up at night.
Yet every clue's a well-timed jest,
For clarity hides while I'm just a guest.

So off I go, on this playful quest,
To find the essence that knows me best.
With every giggle, I lurch and sway,
But laughing with shadows, it's all okay!

Footsteps of Understanding

I tiptoe softly, trying to sneak,
Into a mind that seems quite bleak.
But understanding's a carnival ride,
Where I bump into thoughts and collide!

Each step resounds like a playful dance,
Mistakes are made, but what's the chance?
I laugh and spin, a jovial mime,
Yet clarity plays hide-and-seek each time.

I tried to measure, I pulled a string,
It snapped right back, oh the joy it brings!
With every misstep, I find my thread,
A tangle of thoughts, oh where am I led?

I'll keep on stepping, a goofy glide,
With puzzled looks, but oh, I'll abide.
Every stumble, a reason to grin,
In the footprint game, I'll just dive in!

Beyond the Horizon of Thought

I sail on dreams, a whimsical boat,
Past the horizon, where giggles float.
With every wave, a thought may sprout,
But clarity's never been about doubt!

The stars play tricks, winking at me,
While I juggle notions, so wild and free.
I toss and turn in the cosmic stew,
But understanding dances, always askew!

My brain's a circus, full of clowns,
Each thought a balloon that bounces and frowns.
I reach for answers, grab at the sky,
Yet all I catch is a bird's sly fly.

So here I drift, in this vast expanse,
With a heart that laughs and a silly stance.
I'll chase those thoughts till they land just right,
For beyond the horizon, it's sheer delight!

Slippers of the Sun on a Cloudy Day

In bright yellow shoes, I tripped on a dream,
A sunbeam slipped past, or so it would seem.
Chasing my tail, oh what a delight,
Who knew that the clouds would steal all my light?

With each tiny giggle, I'm slipping and slide,
The laughter echoes, can't help but abide.
Sunshine hides, playing peek-a-boo games,
While I wobble around in my colorful frames.

The socks on my feet are dancing in tune,
That raincloud just laughed, made me look like a loony.
But every soft puddle, a smile on my face,
Jumping right in, oh, what a fun race!

Through laughter and slips, I'm always a step,
Behind that bright giggle, oh how I inept!
So I tiptoe along, in slippers of cheer,
Dancing through life with no sign of fear.

Fading Footprints of Knowledge

I followed a rabbit, with glasses so thick,
He winked and he nodded, I blinked at his trick.
My brain was in chaos, thoughts spinning around,
Like socks in the dryer, they make quite a sound.

I scribbled my notes, then lost them in space,
My pencil's now laughing, oh what a disgrace!
Each thought's like a bubble, they pop and they flee,
Knowledge, it giggles, just out of my reach.

With crayons of wisdom, I doodled and sketched,
But every good scribble just left me bemetched.
Like footprints that fade with a splash of the rain,
My brain does the cha-cha while I scream in vain.

Oh, knowledge, you tease, just out of my grasp,
Like candy on shelves, but I've lost the clasp.
With cookies of reason and sprinkles of fun,
I chase fading footprints, but can't seem to run.

The Chase Through the Thickets of Thought

In a thicket of thoughts, I stumbled on humor,
Like hedgehogs in cartwheels, I fled from a rumor.
Each twist and each turn, I slipped on my wit,
Those branches were giggling, refusing to sit.

I dashed through the bushes, both sneaky and sly,
In fumbles of mind, oh how I did fly!
A wild chase ensued, with squirrels in the lead,
They mocked my pursuit, planted seeds of misdeed.

I tripped on a rabbit, who danced with a grin,
He challenged my focus, let the chaos begin.
I laughed as I tumbled, through thistles and grass,
In thickets of folly, I'm always the class.

So here in my frolic, I chase after glee,
Where thoughts hide and leap, turning wild as can be.
Through paths all confused, let the fun have its say,
I'm happily lost, in this mind's grand ballet.

Tracing the Edge of the Unknowable

With crayons of wonder, I color the air,
Tracing edges of places that never quite share.
Each line leads to laughter, but what's down the road?
A chicken in slippers, in a heavy load!

I peeked at the edges, where laughter won't stop,
The unknowable chuckles, made me miss my hop.
As I mapped out the sky with giggles in flight,
An owl turned his head, gave me quite a fright!

Lost in the curves, I slipped on a rhyme,
Thoughts waltzed around me, just wasting my time.
I chased after shadows, they danced as they ran,
With whispers of secrets no one else ran.

Amidst all the chaos, I draw and I play,
Laughter spills over on this whimsical day.
Each trace of the unknown, a jest and a jest,
In tracing those edges, I find my own quest.

Beyond the Grasp of Logic

In the maze of my thoughts, I chase,
A squirrel named Reason, always in haste.
He giggles and darts, never stays put,
While I trip over my own two feet and scoot.

I ponder and think, my head in a spin,
As facts dance around, taunting me in.
Like a cat with a laser, he's out of my reach,
I swear he's a wizard, he's not one to teach.

I bring out my notebook, I try to draw lines,
But the ink turns to jello, and I draw in designs.
Each plan is a riddle, unwrapped with a shrug,
Logic's a prankster, I'm caught in the mug.

So I'll skip on this path, twirl 'round like a fool,
Where clarity's bright but I'm stuck in the pool.
Maybe tomorrow, I'll catch him for sure,
But today's just a circus, I'm laughing for sure.

The Trail of Unwritten Answers

I seek out the signs that lead to the wise,
But they flicker like fireflies, playing in disguise.
Each question I ask meets a laugh and a shrug,
Like my socks that match poorly, all tangled and snug.

With every new riddle, my head starts to spin,
I scribble down answers with a silly grin.
But my guidebook's a mystery, each page rips apart,
Just fluff and confetti, a true work of art.

Do I chase after hints or do I wait for a clue?
It's a game of charades with a twist or two.
The trees whisper secrets, but they're speaking in rhymes,
I'm lost in the giggles, I'm out of my times.

So here's to the trail where the answers may hide,
I wander and wonder, with laughter as my guide.
Awkwardly dancing on this whimsical track,
The joy is the journey, though I'm never on back.

Slivers of Light in the Abyss

The abyss calls to me, with shadows and cheer,
It tickles my senses, oh dear, oh dear!
With slivers of light that tease at the dark,
I follow the giggles, like a peculiar lark.

Why does wisdom wear polka dots, I ponder?
And why does it vanish just as I wander?
I scrunch up my face, looking left and then right,
The answers are playing a game of hide and fright.

Each turn that I take reveals more of the jest,
Like socks in a dryer, no way to be dressed.
Logic is wrestling with giggles in glee,
While I'm busy tripping over my own knee.

So here I shall sit, with my grin and my wits,
In the light of absurdity, where laughter still fits.
I'll dance in this void, with absurdity's grin,
For finding the answers is where the fun begins.

Searching for the Unseen Map

I'm on the hunt for a map that's unwritten,
With directions that tangle and humor that's smitten.
Each corner I turn, there's a joke waiting there,
A riddle wrapped up in a fluffy gold chair.

The north is a gummy bear, sweet and absurd,
While south is a banana that just hasn't heard.
I take note of the compass—it spins with a laugh,
Pointing me nowhere, just leading a gaffe.

With each step I take, I stumble and weave,
The path is a puzzle, but I choose to believe.
That laughter is wisdom, though it's loose and quite spry,
And these giddy mistakes are where the fun lies nigh.

So I'll quest on this journey, mapless yet bold,
In a world full of giggles, with stories retold.
Finding joy in the chaos, I dance with delight,
For the absurdity shines in the soft moonlight.

Half-formed Thoughts on the Wind

A whisper floats, just out of reach,
Like a cat that won't come near to teach.
I chase it wildly with clumsy grace,
Only to find it's left no trace.

Ideas shimmy in and out of sight,
Like dance partners lost in a spotlight.
I trip on words, and giggle in glee,
As thoughts dart away, pretending to flee.

The Path of Perpetual Pursuit

I run in circles, a dog with a bone,
Chasing my dreams that won't be my own.
I slip on a banana peel of despair,
With every step forward, I'm still unaware.

Each signpost points to paths unknown,
I yell at the map, 'Why's this so overblown?'
The road keeps winding, a comedic twist,
I stop and ponder, but something's amiss.

Threads of Truth Unraveled

I tug at the yarn of scattered thought,
But each frayed end leaves me more distraught.
Kittens play with what I try to weave,
A tapestry of nonsense I can't believe.

I stitch a patch that never will fit,
Reality laughs at my little skit.
The colors clash like an awful dream,
Yet here I am, lost in this meme.

Lost in Interpretation's Maze

I wander through halls of twisted signs,
Each turn takes me where logic unwinds.
Mice with glasses analyze my plight,
While I decode riddles under the moonlight.

Oh, the jokes are plenty and puns abound,
As I stumble blindly, laughing around.
Each corner I find, a farce in disguise,
An endless loop of unforeseen surprise.

The Journey of Silent Questions

Hiking up the mountain of thought,
With a backpack of queries I brought.
Every step's a ponder, a slip or a trip,
On answers just out of reach, I grip.

Each turn is a riddle, a laugh in disguise,
The clouds whisper answers, but still I can't rise.
Why's the sky blue? Does toast really fly?
Oh silly me, it's just my own sigh.

Dancing with doubt on this slippery trail,
My thoughts like a kite, caught by the gale.
I chase after wisdom, it dodges my grasp,
Its cheeky little giggle makes questions unclasp.

Yet in this adventure, I can't help but grin,
For the fun is the journey, not where to begin.
With every misstep, I'm led to the muse,
I stumble on humor, it's mine to peruse.

The Veil of Understanding

Behind a curtain of fog, I peer,
Searching for truths just out of ear.
Whispers of logic float on the breeze,
But tangled in riddles, I'm falling to my knees.

With glasses amiss, I squint and I frown,
Trying to sift through the cobwebbed renown.
What do they mean when they nod and they smile?
I chase their cleverness, but it's fickle all the while.

A jester's cap rests atop of my head,
As I ponder the thoughts that were never quite said.
Cracking the codes like an egg on the floor,
Oh! The yolks of confusion call out for more.

Yet laughter erupts as I bumble along,
In the dance of the absurd, I find I belong.
Each errant step keeps my spirits in flight,
After all, it's the folly that brings forth the light.

Whirlwinds of Forgotten Insight

Whirling thoughts like leaves in the wind,
I chase after knowledge, it's hopelessly pinned.
Round and round in a dizzying spin,
But what have I learned? A chuckle within.

The lightbulb pops, then it flickers, then dies,
As wisdom eludes like my best-friend's replies.
I scribble in circles, it's a riddle in jest,
Finding clarity's art? Well, I'm still just a guest.

A tumbleweed's wisdom rolls idly by,
While I chase after shadows, oh why do I try?
Each twist and each turn leads me back to my door,
With only the echoes of what I implore.

But oh how I laugh at this marvelous game,
Like a clown chasing answers, it's all just the same.
In whirlwinds of insight, I spiral and play,
For the joy of the chase is what brightens my day.

The Chase Through a Never-ending Labyrinth

In the maze of confusion, I sprint and I dart,
With walls made of questions, they're tough on the heart.
Each corner I turn shows a new set of clues,
But the more that I chase, the more I still lose.

The Minotaur's laugh echoes deep in the hall,
As I stumble on riddles that trip and befall.
With breadcrumbs of reason, I map out my quest,
Yet each path I take seems to lead to the jest.

A hedgehog in disguise, it teases and rolls,
While I chase my own tail, oh what are my goals?
For every great answer, a dozen more sprout,
And I huff and I puff, feeling lost in a rout.

But still there's a giggle that bubbles inside,
For the chase is the fun, there's no need to hide.
So round and round through this puzzle I bound,
Finding joy in the journey, where laughter is found.

Forbidden Questions Under Starlight

Why does the moon wear a frown?
It's just a big cheese in a gown.
My thoughts dance like fireflies bright,
While squirrels plot crimes in the night.

Questions pop like corn on a stove,
Like why does my cat think it's a grove?
Hidden truths swirl in the breeze,
As my shoes trip over the trees.

Constellations wink as they tease,
While I ponder life's mystery with ease.
Who knew a star could giggle so loud?
I'm lost in the dark but feeling proud.

So come join me, twirl around,
Chasing questions that won't be found.
Underneath this cosmic dome,
Let's laugh at the things we can't call home.

Between the Word and the Whisper

There's a word stuck in my throat,
It's wearing a very silly coat.
Whispers wiggle with giggly glee,
Like jellybeans bouncing from a spree.

Between the 'what' and 'why' I roam,
Chasing shadows that won't come home.
Do frogs really laugh in a pond?
Or is it just me being fond?

I ask the clouds if they feel blue,
They chuckle, say "That's just for you!"
My thoughts are like butterflies on the run,
Always playing tag in the sun.

So let's twirl 'round these puzzling sounds,
Silly questions flying like hounds.
For every whisper, there's a jest,
And in this giggle, we're truly blessed.

Searching for Solace in Solitude

Solitude's a quirky friend,
Dancing wildly, it'll never end.
I seek solace in a sea of socks,
Wondering if they have clocks.

Every corner's filled with my thoughts,
Wrestling with invisible knots.
Do shadows wear shoes when they walk?
Or is that aimed just for talk?

Couch cushions hold secrets untold,
Of past laughs and moments bold.
I together with my quirky chair,
Share stories floatin' in the air.

So if you find me sipping tea,
With a book that's gone all spree,
Just know laughter's my only goal,
In this silent, chaotic stroll.

Untangling the Web of Thoughts

Thoughts are like spaghetti on a plate,
Twisting and turning, they just can't wait.
Why does my brain like to trip?
On dreams that flip in a wild skip?

I ponder the dance of a wayward ant,
Moving to rhythms, though they can't chant.
Will I ever catch the thoughts I loose?
Or will they run wild, like a moose?

Tangled webs that shimmer and twine,
Wrap 'round ideas that subtly shine.
I stand confused, scratching my head,
Are these the thoughts that the cats said?

So here's to the chaos of silly thoughts,
Each one's a puzzle, and boy, they're hot!
With laughter as my guiding light,
I'll untangle this web every night.

Wandering in the Weeds of Reflection

In a garden where thoughts grow wild,
I search for wisdom like a lost child.
Each flower shouts, 'Look at me!'
While I stumble over a bumblebee.

The sun tickles my thoughts so bright,
But the rabbit laughs, 'You're not quite right!'
I scratch my head, feeling a bit dense,
As the daisies plot to build a fence.

A caterpillar offers me advice,
Saying, 'Slow down, it's not a race!'
I nod, but he's munching on a leaf,
While I ponder life's seasonal grief.

As I wander through this patchy maze,
The weeds whisper secrets in a haze.
Yet I leave with a smile, feeling absurd,
For the nature of thought's always a blur.

Echoes in the Hall of Dreams

In a hallway where shadows tease,
I question myself, with giggles and wheezes.
Ghosts of ideas float silently,
Trying to catch me, quite violently.

I chase after them, they slip away,
Like fish on a line, they dance and play.
One says, 'Why chase when you can nap?'
I reply, 'Nah! Dreams should wear a cap!'

Suddenly a door creaks open wide,
And in strolls a cat with nothing to hide.
He grins at me, says, 'Silly human,
Try chasing tails or watch the moonman!'

But I skedaddle off into the night,
With echoes of laughter fading from sight.
Was it a dream, or just plain fun?
In the hall, the uncertainty's never done.

The Heart's Relentless Pursuit

My heart runs faster than a kid on candy,
Chasing after thoughts, oh so dandy.
But every corner hides a twist,
And it figures out I'm lost in mist.

I trip over feelings like a clown on a stage,
Every step is marked by a funny page.
'Catch me if you can!' my heart does shout,
While I'm caught thinking thoughts too loud.

It dodges left, then jigs to the right,
I'm a spectator in this comical fight.
A dance of joy and awkward flair,
While my heart just laughs; I live in despair!

But I'll not give up, oh no not me,
I'll grab a balloon and set my heart free!
With each chase, I find more glee,
In this wild pursuit of pure jubilee.

The Path Less Grasped

Walking on a path that bends and sways,
I find my thoughts in a joyful malaise.
Every stone tries to tell a tale,
But I'm stuck in the web of a lackluster snail.

The trees shake their heads, whisper, 'please!,'
'You'll find more fun beneath the leaves!'
Yet here I stand, with a crooked grin,
Trying to coax a squirrel to come in.

It's not the road that leads to grand sights,
But a trail of laughter that ignites the nights.
I trip on my shoelaces, tumble and roll,
But oh what a joy to lose full control!

So I'll march on this unpredictable ride,
With squirrels for company, right by my side.
In the end, it seems, I grasped the jest,
In this wobbly dance, I found my best.

A Symphony of Unanswered Searches

In the quest for joy, I trip on a shoe,
My coffee's gone cold, it says, "Oops, not for you!"
I chase laughter like it's a runaway cat,
But it swerves to the left, and then just falls flat.

I ask for directions, they point with a grin,
To where I should go, but I can't find my skin.
The map's upside down, or was it me all along?
I dance in confusion, but still sing my song.

My thoughts are like socks, always lost in the wash,
A mix-up of colors, a puzzling quench to quash.
I search for a joke, but it's hiding so sly,
I shrug to the mirror, just let out a sigh.

So here's to the chaos, the laughs and the fumbles,
Life's a grand circus where logic just stumbles.
With a wink and a nudge, I'm still in the race,
Just me and my giggles, in this baffling place.

Footprints in the Fog

In the morning mist, I lose track of my shoes,
In a game of hide-and-seek, I'm bound to lose.
The fog rolls in thick, like a warm, fuzzy blanket,
I look for the path, but it's as lost as a planet.

I step on a puddle, splash everywhere, dear,
Turns out it's a mirage, where's my sense of cheer?
With slippers for boots, I storm through the haze,
My thoughts march in circles, like squirrels in a daze.

Each twist of the breeze pulls me further astray,
Is my coffee still brewing? I hope saves the day.
I try for a laugh, but it's muffled in gray,
Where whispers of punchlines just quietly sway.

Yet I wade through the fog, as I dance to the beat,
With each tiny misstep, I find life bittersweet.
In the chaos of choices, I find quite the spell,
Who needs all the answers when I'm laughing so well?

Elusive Echoes of Thought

Sitting in silence, my brain starts to race,
Thoughts scatter like leaves in a whimsical chase.
I ponder a riddle but laugh at the twist,
When it slips through my fingers, will it be missed?

A glance at my notebook, the scribbles all dance,
Like ants in a picnic, they're here by mere chance.
I tried to remember a punchline or two,
Then tripped on the patio, fell right into blue.

Echoes of questions bounce straight off the wall,
I stumble on answers, but can't catch them all.
Sometimes I feel wisdom is just out of view,
But what's life without giggles, and moments askew?

I chase down my thoughts, like a dog with a stick,
But they zigzag away, oh, what a neat trick!
In laughter and flounders, I find my own way,
Here's to all echoes that just want to play!

Chasing Shadows in Twilight

In twilight's soft glow, my shadow's a prank,
I stroll with my thoughts, but they flip and they yank.
Each curve of the path feels like a surprise,
I laugh at my shadow, we're both full of lies.

With a hop and a skip, I chase it real tight,
It's weaving through trees, oh what a sly sight!
It ducks and it dives, like it's playing tag,
Each twist that it takes makes my humor just wag.

I ponder my choices, but they vanish like mist,
What dance steps to take? It's all on the list.
The stars peek above with a twinkle and grin,
As they giggle at me, the night's just begun.

In the chase of the dark, I find silly delight,
Though shadows may flee, I'll keep laughing all night.
For in every small flounder, joy's always the prize,
With a wink and a sway, I'm onward I rise!

Whispers of Wisdom in the Dark

In shadows where I trip and fall,
A sage's laugh, I hear it call.
With every twist, a riddle flies,
I scratch my head and scan the skies.

The lightbulb flickers, then goes out,
I grin and ponder all about.
Each hint I chase just slips away,
As wisdom dances, starts to sway.

A quirky joke in every thought,
I leap for answers I have sought.
But every time I punch the clock,
The punchline's gone, it leaves me shocked.

So here I stand, with twists and turns,
In laughter's grip, my spirit yearns.
The night grows dim, yet I must try,
To catch that gleam that flies on by.

The Dance of Ambiguity

In a circle, doubts do twirl,
Logic spins, but thoughts unfurl.
I try to lead this comical dance,
Yet slip on words that twist my stance.

A step to left, then suddenly right,
The rhythm shifts, gives me a fright.
Giggles echo, confusion's queen,
As clarity plays hide-and-seek, unseen.

I juggle phrases, twist and shout,
No straightforward path to route.
In every turn, a chuckle grows,
Ambiguity has its funny shows.

I leap with hope, I stake my claim,
But logic laughs, it plays its game.
In this dance of whimsy and cheer,
I'll trip for joy, not quake in fear.

Always Just Out of Reach

Like a carrot on a stick so bright,
I chase the answer, full of might.
With every sprint, it stays afar,
A laughing moon, a teasing star.

I leap with glee, a wild-eyed fetch,
Only to find, it's a game of etch.
I'm stuck in circles, round and round,
In giggles lost, no answer found.

It winks at me from yonder hill,
A flash of genius, oh what a thrill!
But when I reach, it fades away,
A playful ghost that loves to play.

So here I stand with thoughts galore,
I laugh aloud and ask for more.
For though the chase may leave me sore,
The fun of seeking I adore.

Echoes of Insight Above

In lofty realms, ideas soar,
They tease my mind, then shut the door.
A whisper here, a giggle there,
My thoughts, it seems, are light as air.

The sky is full of cheeky dreams,
As insights play their sneaky schemes.
With every leap, I grasp at clouds,
Only to laugh amid the crowds.

I chase the echoes of delight,
They beckon me to join their flight.
On wings of jest, they flit and flair,
I'm left below, in joyous despair.

Yet still I grin, not lost to gloom,
For every thought creates its bloom.
The echoes ring with laughter bright,
In playful tones, they spark the night.

The Intersection of Insight and Ambiguity

At the crossing where thoughts collide,
A sign says 'turn left' but I slide.
Clarity's a game, I can't quite win,
Chasing the rabbit, I grin and spin.

With each twist, my logic grows dim,
I ask questions, answers on a whim.
Like a cat chasing a laser beam,
What's reality? Just a funny dream.

Traffic lights flash, they taunt my brain,
Every green light feels like a strain.
In the chaos, I try to straddle,
Finding the path in this wild rattle.

But no GPS for thoughts afoul,
I honk at shadows; my mind's a howl.
At the intersection, I laugh in glee,
As insight plays hide and seek with me.

Fathoming the Depths of Ambivalence

Diving deep where thoughts don't settle,
I find more questions, it's a riddle kettle.
One moment up, next I'm down,
Wearing a smile, then a frown.

Like juggling eggs while riding a bike,
My mind's an adventure, yikes! What a hike!
Ambivalence? I'll take a slice,
In this soup of life, it ain't so nice.

With each gulp, I taste the fog,
A dog chasing tails, just a smog.
In the depths, I try to steer,
But clarity swims just out of here.

Bubbles pop, and I burst with laughter,
Searching for wisdom, but finding a chapter.
In confusion's dance, I twirl and sway,
What a circus! Now, where's my way?

The Infinite Run for Meaning

On a treadmill of thoughts, I jog in place,
Chasing a thought like a game of chase.
With every step, I'm running fast,
But meaning's a mirage, never to last.

Like a hamster in wheels, round and round,
I search for answers that can't be found.
Sprinters give chase, but I just walk,
Catching the whispers, I hear them talk.

Jogging through questions with joy and dread,
Each laugh a companion, each giggle well-fed.
Tripping on syllables, I stumble and roll,
The finish line's clear, yet I'm still on a stroll.

So I laugh at the chase, this peculiar race,
With no map in hand, I'm lost in the space.
But oh, what a journey! I yell out with cheer,
In the infinite run, the fun's oh so near!

Reflections from the Mirror of Perception

Stand before the glass, what do I see?
A jester's face looking back at me.
With each reflection, I grin and twist,
Reality's punchline I can't resist.

The mirror chuckles, "You're quite the sight!"
I dance with shadows, embracing the light.
Searching for answers in each silly stare,
Caught in the whims of who's really there.

Images distort, a carnival fun,
I'm juggling reflections, one by one.
A tangle of smiles, a riddle to crack,
In this funny house, who's losing track?

So I laugh with the glass, as it laughs back,
Life's just a sketch on an ink-smeared track.
In the mirror's embrace, I find a friend,
In this puzzle of vision, the laughs never end.

The Intrigue of Invisible Processes

I ponder hard, it slips away,
Like socks that vanish, day by day.
I chase the thoughts that tease and play,
A comedy of errors on display.

My coffee's cold, my brain's on fire,
A jester's dance, my grand desire.
With every step, I seem to tire,
Where clarity exists, I misconspire.

Each riddle wraps in stealthy disguise,
Like squirrels that plot, with gleeful eyes.
I trip through life, the jokester cries,
For wisdom's paired with cartoonish lies.

Each question springs, a mirthful tease,
A circus act beneath tall trees.
While I'll bust limbs, knees full of freeze,
I'll laugh it off, with perfect ease.

Gossamer Threads of Understanding

I grasp at thoughts, they tickle my wit,
Like spiders spinning random bits.
In webs of nonsense, I'll happily sit,
Seeking laughter, not a perfect fit.

At every turn, confusion reigns,
Like juggling pies on runaway trains.
A circus clown, I hold my reins,
With giggles shared, it softly pains.

We dance with questions, bold and spry,
Like acrobats in a comical fly.
Logic's a squirrel, so spry, oh my!
Diving for nuts, but oh, so shy.

Entangled threads, a playful sight,
With goofy grins, we'll take our flight.
Though answers hide, just out of sight,
In funny echoes, we find delight.

A Glimpse Beyond the Fog

In clouds of doubt, I squint and peer,
A blurry vision, yet full of cheer.
The world is wild, but who's in the rear?
As fog rolls in, we hold our beer.

I twist and turn like a clown on stage,
With every blink, I feel the age.
Each thought a cat, uncaged in rage,
It prances around, my inner mage.

A slippery slope, I slide with glee,
Teetering on the edge, so free.
Like rubber chickens in a tree,
I bumble through, oh woe is me!

Yet something brews behind the haze,
With comical quirks and silly ways.
I'll take the plunge, embrace the maze,
Laughing off this foggy phase.

Fragments of a Deeply Absurd Puzzle

Pieces scattered, munching crumbs,
I search in vain for dreadful sums.
Like jigsaw pieces turned to bums,
In a kiddie pool of giggles, it hums.

With every guess, I miss the mark,
Like trying to fish in a city park.
Clown cars zoom with giddy spark,
Oh, this absurdity, quite the lark!

Riddles chase me, zigzag and spin,
A carnival ride, let the fun begin.
The punchline's lost, where have I been?
Each tangled thought, a cheeky grin.

Yet in this mess, a truth does gleam,
A jester's dance, a wild dream.
We'll laugh and shout, a perfect team,
In fragments we find our shared meme.

Fragments of Revelation

In the morning, thoughts collide,
Like ducks trying to stay aligned.
Each idea flaps and flails,
Chasing wisdom like a dog on trails.

Where did my thoughts get away?
In the fridge or out to play?
I open doors with pins and keys,
To find the joke, but not the cheese.

Between the tangle of my mind,
A giggling ghost, so hard to find.
It plays hide and seek, I'll pursue,
But all it leaves is quite the view!

So here's to the puzzle, silly and bright,
As I tumble through clouds, what a sight.
In fragments they shine, but oh the catch!
With every laugh, they're hard to snatch.

In the Shadow of My Queries

Questions loom like cats in trees,
Curious, yet tricky with ease.
I call to them, come down, I dare,
But they just giggle, float in air.

Chasing shadows with a net,
Every corner holds a pet.
Just when I think I'm in the zone,
A rubber chicken takes the throne!

Pondering deeply, I scratch my head,
Am I awake or curled in bed?
The answers play hopscotch with my brain,
Laughter and confusion, quite the game!

So I sit here, questions like confetti,
A parade of nonsense, always ready.
Each answer a balloon that floats away,
I'll grab a cake; let's celebrate this play!

Tracing the Lines of Revelation

I doodle dreams on dinner plates,
While pondering why this math awaits.
The fork I use, a wand of fate,
Turns soup into a number plate!

Tracing lines with forks and spoons,
I draw odd shapes, becoming loons.
With every slurp, the patterns shift,
A culinary art that gives me a lift.

I paint with ketchup, search for signs,
While spaghetti dances, twirling vines.
The sauce spills secrets, and I just grin,
A masterpiece of chaos, let's begin!

Through every bite a puzzle shared,
In the flavor, a riddle dared.
With laughter, I dip in and out,
What did I chase? I have my doubts!

The Riddle That Eludes Me

A riddle tips its hat and grins,
As I chase it around with playful spins.
It giggles softly, dodging my gaze,
And dances away in a foggy haze.

Like socks that vanish in the wash,
This riddle makes me feel quite posh.
It teases me from behind the couch,
And squeaks like mice when I try to slouch.

In every corner, it leaves a clue,
A funny face, a silly boo!
But when I leap, it hops away,
Leaving me to chuckle, day by day.

So here I am, on this merry chase,
With laughter following, at a quick pace.
The riddle stays just out of reach,
Yet the joy it brings? Oh, it's quite a speech!

Ever Out of Reach

I stretch my arms, they pull away,
Like kittens on a sunny day.
I chase my thoughts, they dance and sway,
At twilight's dusk, they go astray.

I ask a question, it teases back,
In riddles wrapped, it's lost the track.
It giggles softly, on a snack,
And leaves me here, a mental wreck.

The answers hide, they play a game,
They change their outfits, never tame.
Each time I swear I'll stake my claim,
Yet they slip past me, what a shame!

So on I go, mismatched and mad,
A comic tale of good and bad.
With every twist, I find I'm glad,
For laughter's here, it's not so sad.

Battling the Current of Illusion

I float along the riverwide,
With questions in a boat I ride.
The current pulls, I'm quite the guide,
Yet here I sit, I turn, I'm tied.

I throw a line to catch my thought,
It dances like it wants to trot.
I reel it in, but what I've caught,
Is just a fish made of a plot.

With every wave, the dreams collide,
I wave my fists; they slip and slide.
I shout for truth, it laughs and hides,
While ducks and doubts join in the ride.

But oh, this journey has its fun,
With silly tales by river run.
In chasing light, I find the pun,
And wander on till day is done.

The Seeker's Dilemma

I search for clues beneath my bed,
With socks and crumbs and thoughts I thread.
What did I lose? Can't find my head,
The mystery of the missing lead.

I ask the cat, she twitches ears,
She blinks at me, avoids my fears.
With every meow, she steers my peers,
Towards tangled thoughts and ancient beers.

Oh seeker's path is paved with jest,
With clever signs that leave me pressed.
I chase the lark, it seems the best,
Yet all I gain is mental zest.

But laughter brings a light so bright,
To question why I'm chasing light.
In all this chaos, feels just right,
I'll find my way, with pure delight.

Journeys without Destination

I pack my bags with dreams and snacks,
Set off to find the mystic tracks.
Each turn I take, my logic cracks,
As nonsense leads my brain to relax.

I wander through a field of whim,
With butterflies that dance and swim.
A signpost points, my vision's dim,
Yet every chance seems just a whim.

The map I drew's an endless reel,
A tangle of what might reveal.
I spin and twirl, I laugh and squeal,
For every lost is now a steal.

Though paths may twist and truths may turn,
In every loss, there's much to learn.
I greet the madness, let it burn,
Each step I take, a new concern.

The Puzzle Without a Picture

A jigsaw missing half the pieces,
Edges are sharp, but oh, where's the lease?
I guess it's all in how you see,
Maybe it's just a cat set free.

I turn it this way, then that, oh dear,
A duck, a fish, or perhaps a sneer?
It's like I'm solving while sipping beer,
No real answers, just a raucous cheer.

My brain's a maze, to my surprise,
Each twist and turn unveils new lies.
Rearranged thoughts like circus flies,
And still no clue where the puzzle lies.

In a box marked "No Clue" I reside,
Swinging left, then right, with hopeful pride.
I'll put it together, just you bide,
Winners get cake, come join my ride!

Inkblots of Uncertainty

A splash of color, what do I see?
A goat in a suit, or just a tree?
The psychologist laughs, can't disagree,
"Just scribbles," he says, "but it's all free."

In my mind's eye, chaos reigns supreme,
Are all these blots just part of a dream?
Perhaps they're puzzles, or maybe a scheme,
Creating an art that's more than it seems.

I ponder deep, take the ink with a sip,
What's underneath, is it a cryptic script?
The doctor is puzzled, his coffee I tip,
We laugh at the nonsense, let wisdom slip.

With every blot, I see deeper layers,
Each looks like jelly on crusty containers.
Here's an elephant, next to some sprayers,
Inkblots are blank, just our silly players.

Between the Lines of Understanding

Words upon words, a twinkling dance,
Pauses and laughter, might give a chance.
Read between lines, or wear the wrong pants,
Either way, love's got an odd romance.

I scribble messages, but fate's a tease,
Caught in translations, my brain's on a freeze.
Loaded with meaning, yet feeling such ease,
I'm picking daisies while dodging the bees.

When clarity strikes, it's hidden from view,
I ask for directions, they point to the zoo.
My head's filled with notions that swirl and stew,
In a sea of confusion, I'm lost, who knew?

With giggles and grins, I chase what I sought,
In circles I spin, with thoughts that are fraught.
But humor's the compass, guiding my plot,
Between the lines, who's lost? I forgot!

The Mirage of Comprehension

A desert of thoughts, I wander around,
Chasing a vision, but where's it found?
A mirage of wisdom on shifting ground,
Tickling my brain, no truth can be crowned.

I reach for rocks that turn to sweet sand,
Logic is fleeting, it slips from my hand.
Fool's gold glimmers, as dreams expand,
Narratives spin like a marching band.

Where's the punchline? Did I miss the cue?
A cactus is laughing, a real hoot, it's true.
Here's my pretzel of thoughts, all anew,
In this land of mirage, there's laughter in view.

But as I trek on, embracing the fun,
I'll dance with the mirage, until I'm done.
With a wink to the world and a quirky pun,
In this fool's paradise, we all can run!

Mapping the Soul's Questions

In the maze of my mind's delight,
Quesions bounce like a kite in flight.
I chase them round, they giggle and flee,
I trip on the thoughts, so slippery!

With every twist, my brain does pirouette,
Like a jester in fog, never to fret.
In laughter, I find that just one wise clue,
Is a slippery pancake, with syrup that flew!

A compass spins wildly, oh what a show!
It points to the sky, but I need it below.
With a chuckle I note, where's the coffee stand?
For questions are plenty, yet thirst is quite grand!

The map's just a doodle, with scribbles galore,
Leading me nowhere, but still I explore.
Each answer eludes me, like socks in the wash,
Yet laughter is gold, so I never say posh!

Threads of Thought Unraveled

A ball of yarn rolls, my brain's craft in play,
Threads of my musings all tangled away.
I pull at a string, oh what a surprise!
A bewildered thought pops up right before my eyes!

Each stitch is a question, a knot in the way,
I tug on a query, and the colors display.
With every pull, laughter winds through the air,
As I knit every thought, with misplaced flair!

The fabric of genius is stitched with a grin,
But the pattern is faulty, could chaos begin?
I roll up my sleeves, let's weave something bright,
A quilt of confusion, a beautiful fright!

So if you see me, with yarn in a twist,
Just smile and join in – you won't want to miss.
For in this odd tapestry where quirks are styled,
Even quandaries tickle, each question beguiled!

Quandaries of the Curious Heart

Oh, the heart's a riddle, a puzzle so sly,
It flutters and flops, like a fish out to fly.
With questions that tease, it leads me astray,
While I laugh and I wonder, will I find my way?

Each beat's a dilemma, a chuckle or sigh,
Is love an illusion or just pie in the sky?
I ponder and ponder, with a wink and a cheer,
Yet the heart finds its way, it's funny, my dear!

In the carnival of feelings, oh what a ride,
With cotton candy hopes that bubble inside.
Each thought drips like syrup, a sugary mess,
Leaving trails of giggles, like a sweet-hearted quest!

So I dance with my doubts, with a grin and a twirl,
For each curious question's a treat to unfurl.
The heart's not for solving, but savoring fun,
In all of its quirks, my answers outrun!

The Uncharted Territory of the Mind

In the wild of my brain, where oddities sprout,
Thoughts roam like critters, full of giggles and doubt.
Each corner I turn, a surprise awaits me,
With a wink from the muse, oh what could it be?

Maps drawn with crayons, chaotic and bright,
Show paths to nowhere, yet sparkle with light.
With every misstep, I trip on a whim,
And snort with laughter, as I play on the brim!

Oh, the jungles of knowledge, so dense and so wide,
With vines made of questions, in fun we abide.
I swing from my ponderings, a monkey in glee,
In the land of the curious, I'm wild and I'm free!

So join me, dear traveler, in this comical quest,
Where thoughts are a circus, and laughter's the best.
For in this wild wonder, we'll chuckle and roam,
In the uncharted terrain, we'll find our way home!

The Quest for Clarity

I chased a thought, it turned to smoke,
Like catching fish while telling jokes.
The answers danced just out of reach,
While I pondered life upon the beach.

My brain, a maze of silly games,
Confused by logic's silly claims.
The clarity was dressed in stripes,
A zebra prancing, oh so hype!

I thought I'd found the golden key,
A treasure map to set me free.
But every turn just led to fun,
A wild goose chase—who needs to run?

So here I am with questions grand,
On simple shores with a sifting hand.
The quest for clarity still calls,
As I trip over my own shoelaces and falls.

Fleeting Whispers of Truth

The truth appeared in a bright balloon,
It floated past, a cheerful tune.
I tried to grab it, but oh, it teased,
Like that last cookie, just popped and wheezed.

I asked a cat, "What do you know?"
He blinked at me, put on a show.
His wisdom was a purring spree,
But still, no answers came to me.

The whispers giggled, darted fast,
Like shadows danced in shadows cast.
I followed closely, almost there—
But trivial thoughts were all I'd share.

So I'll sip tea and watch the sky,
While fleeting truths just pass me by.
I'll chuckle soft, I'll laugh with glee,
As clarity continues to flee.

Understanding on the Horizon

I peered through binoculars, hoping to see,
Understanding smiling back at me.
But all I got was a lowly bird,
That chirped a nonsense, how absurd!

I climbed a hill and waved a flag,
But all I found was an old, gray rag.
It flapped and flopped, a cheeky prank,
While truth hid deeper in the tank.

The sunrise promised golden chance,
Yet I stumbled, tripped in my dance.
The horizon chuckled, wore a grin,
As I sprawled out, still seeking within.

But tomorrow's light will surely show,
The mysteries wrapped in jesting flow.
With a wink from fate, I'll find my way,
To understanding's curious play.

The Dance of Distant Insights

They twirled and spun, those distant sights,
Like fireflies in the summer nights.
With every leap, I felt the tease,
A game of tag, like playful breeze.

I tried to join, but tripped on air,
Those insights laughed, as if to dare.
"Catch us if you can!" they shrieked in fun,
But I just laughed, still on the run.

The music played, a silly tune,
I danced against the rising moon.
Each step was met with giggles bright,
Insanity wrapped in sheer delight.

So let them laugh and take their flight,
I'll revel in the dimming light.
The dance goes on, and I will sway,
To distant insights that drift away.

www.ingramcontent.com/pod-product-compliance
Lightning Source LLC
Chambersburg PA
CBHW071849160426
43209CB00003B/479